THE LONG WAY HOME

THE LONG WAY HOME

SPIRITUAL HELP WHEN SOMEONE YOU LOVE HAS A STROKE

HARRY ALEXANDER COLE

WJKP

Westminster/John Knox Press
Louisville, Kentucky

Scripture quotations from the Revised Standard Version of the Bible are copyrighted 1946, 1952, © 1971, 1973 by the Division of Christian Education of the National Council of the Churches of Christ in the U.S.A. and are used by permission.

Book design by Gene Harris

First edition

Published by Westminster/John Knox Press
Louisville, Kentucky

PRINTED IN THE UNITED STATES OF AMERICA

9 8 7 6 5 4 3 2 1

Library of Congress Cataloging-in-Publication Data

Cole, Harry Alexander, 1943–
    The long way home : spiritual help when someone you love has a stroke / Harry Alexander Cole. — 1st. ed.
        p.   cm.
    Bibliography: p.
    ISBN 0-664-21881-4
    1. Consolation. 2. Cerebrovascular disease—Religious aspects—
Christianity. 3. Cerebrovascular disease—Patients—Family
relationships. 4. Cerebrovascular disease—Patients—Religious
life. I. Title.
BV4905.2.C65 1989
242'.4—dc20   89-33543
                                                        CIP

Dedication

In honor of my mother

In memory of my father

CONTENTS

PREFACE
AND ACKNOWLEDGMENTS

When stroke occurs in a family it affects everyone, not just the victim. Recovery from stroke can become a family experience involving the victim's spouse, siblings, parents, and children. In most instances the burden of responsibility falls on a primary caregiver who will make great sacrifices of time and energy to assist in her or his loved one's return to health. Often, however, as patient and caregiver continue to work toward recovery, the caregiver's own needs get lost in the process and she or he becomes physically, emotionally, and spiritually exhausted.

The purpose of this book is to provide caregivers with a source of spiritual strength as they learn to cope and eventually overcome the devastating effects of stroke for themselves. It seeks to affirm God's healing power in the occurrence and recovery from stroke and the belief that God can redeem even the worst events of our lives and make all things new.

In this book I have interwoven the stories of two patients and their spouses. One patient is a younger woman and the other an older man, so that readers in varying circumstances will be able to identify with the meditations and the concerns expressed.

I wish to acknowledge and thank those who helped

in creating this book: the members of the Baltimore Stroke Club and the Return Program at Sinai Hospital in Baltimore for sharing their stories with me to serve as the basis for the devotional material; Thaddeus P. Pula, M.D., and James J. Lannon, Executive Director of the National Stroke Association, for verifying the accuracy of the medical terminology and information referring to stroke; my secretary, Louise Bailey, for typing the manuscript; my editor at Westminster/John Knox Press, Harold Twiss, for his valuable insight and suggestions for improving the text; and, finally, my wife, Jacqueline, who is my inspiration in all things— and whose own triumph over stroke encouraged me to write this book to begin with.

ONE

STROKE EVENT

HAVING A LITTLE SPELL

Today was the second time I noticed it, Lord.
All of a sudden, in the midst of explaining
  how he was going to refinish the old
  Queen Anne table in the basement,
  he stopped, just for a moment or two,
  and stared at me with this strange
  blank expression across his face.

It was as if he didn't remember anything
  of what he was talking about.
It was like stepping out of time for a while!
  The action stopped:
  he didn't speak,
  I didn't listen;
  he couldn't speak,
  I couldn't listen.
It was strange and scary, God.

When it was over and he came back to reality
I jokingly asked him where he had been.
He had this puzzled and frightened look
  and said he didn't know where he'd been
  or what had happened.
I tried to shrug it off, God, and chalk it up
  to what my grandmother used to call
  "having a little spell."
He tried to do the same, telling me all over again
  how he was going to refinish the table
  and find two matching chairs for it
  at an antique store.
But even as I watched and listened to him, God,
  I wondered to myself . . .
Why did this happen a second time
  and what does it mean?

Peace I leave with you; my peace I give to you; not as the world gives do I give to you. Let not your hearts be troubled, neither let them be afraid.

John 14:27

Great God, let us know how much you care about our worries and our needs. Help us to cast our burdens and our lot in life upon you in faith and hope.

CVA—WHAT IS THAT?

Lord, I've heard this term before:
  cardiovascular accident.
Is that what stroke is? An accident?
It must be! This couldn't happen on purpose!
One minute we were sitting down together talking
  over morning coffee,
  and the next minute he couldn't talk at all
  and the paramedics came and rushed him off
  to the hospital.
I heard one of them say "stroke" on the radio
  as they were leaving.

If this is an accident, God, then someone has made
  a terrible mistake.
And someone is at fault, but who?
Is it you? Or is it him? Or me?
Lord, everything has happened so fast.
I don't know what is going on.
Please help me.

God is our refuge and strength, a very present help
  in trouble.
Therefore we will not fear though the earth should
  change,
  though the mountains shake in the heart of the
  sea . . .
The LORD of hosts is with us;
  the God of Jacob is our refuge.

Psalm 46:1–2, 7

*Lord, be known to all of us in times of trouble; in all
sudden and powerful changes in our lives, be our
strength and refuge.*

THE RIDE IN THE AMBULANCE

I remember riding in a police car once, Lord.
I was the key witness in a trial involving
    a hit-and-run accident.
I was late for court, so we sped down the interstate
    with the siren blaring and lights flashing.
I made it in time and my side won
    because of my testimony.

It was exciting then, God, but this is dreadful.
Not thirty minutes ago my wife passed out
    before me in my arms.
She said she had a headache and was very cold
    and then she was gone.
And now the sirens are wailing and my
    head is spinning and the ambulance is
    bouncing us back and forth as it rolls
    over bumps and potholes in the city's streets
    on the way to the nearest hospital.

We left late, after sitting in front of our house
    for ten minutes.
They said the hospital had to get ready for her
    because her case was special.
God, this must be really serious,
    and if it is so special
    why couldn't they get her there more quickly?
Why did we have to wait?

She's just lying here, God,
    while I hold her head in my hands
    and stroke her cheeks with my fingers.
She feels so cold and won't respond to anything I do.
Her chest seems to hardly rise and fall
    even though she wears an oxygen mask.

Her face is flushed, as when she loses her temper
   with the children or with me.
And yet, there's no expression on her face—
   no anger, no ecstasy, nothing.

The only emotions I am aware of
   are my own: fear, confusion, and
   increased foreboding of what is to come.

What has happened, God?
What is to come?

Be strong and of good courage, do not fear or be in
dread of them: for it is the LORD your God who goes
with you; he will not fail you or forsake you.

Deuteronomy 31:6

*God, help us in times of sudden trouble to lift up our
hearts to you and keep our minds stayed on your words
of guidance and comfort.*

PRESSING THE BUTTON,
HANDLING EMERGENCIES

There is a large red button on the wall
    outside the emergency entrance of the hospital, God.
The paramedics pressed it as they wheeled him
    into the waiting room.
The door flew open with a terrifying crash,
    an ominous welcome to what awaited us inside.
I followed them in, and that's when I first saw
    the chaos and confusion.
I felt another button trip inside of me
    and the panic started all over again.

There are so many strange people here, God.
There are patients who look like accident victims
    and are crying out for help.
There are others who seem to have been fighting
    and need their bones set and their cuts stitched up.
There are doctors and nurses and x-ray technicians
    scurrying about, looking for patient files
    and people to treat.
There are police, ambulance drivers, street people
    with nowhere else to go, and several others
    just standing around watching.
And then there is my husband, lying on a gurney
    along the wall of the hospital corridor.
I look at him and see the fear and confusion
    in his eyes, and I look desperately around for help.
There's no one around; it's as if no one knows
    we have arrived.
Didn't they call to say we were coming?
Don't they know we are here?
Here we are in the midst of all these emergencies!
Isn't there somebody, Lord, who will tend to ours?

This must seem commonplace to those who work here.
I guess everything falls into a routine,
    even handling emergencies.
But for him and for me this is real,
    and we need help.
Please send help, God.
Send it now.

Out of the depths I cry to thee, O LORD!
                                        Psalm 130:1

Eternal God, may you be the way and the truth and the life for us forever.

GETTING THE FACTS STRAIGHT

A nurse finally came and wheeled him to
    the treatment area of the emergency room, Lord.
I stood there and watched him go, and then someone
    said to sit down and wait until my name was called.

I heard my name over the loudspeaker;
    I thought it was news of my husband.
But no—I had to check in with the person
    who handles the paperwork.
I sat down across from her in a small cubicle;
    there was a desk and a large computer between us.
She looked at it, not at me, and punched the keys
    while asking me for information.
Husband's name? Address? Age? Medicare number?
Religion? Family doctor? Been here before?
Blue Cross? Blue Shield? . . .
At last, the questions over, she handed me a form
    to sign in several places,
    to ensure payment for his treatment.

God, this is cruel.
Doesn't she care?
Doesn't she know what suffering goes on here?
My husband is desperately ill,
    and all she seems to care about
    is getting the facts straight in her computer
    to guarantee that the hospital will be paid.
Can she guarantee that the hospital
    will make him well?
I guess we all have our jobs to do—
    this is hers, and she does it well enough.
I signed the forms in all the right places.

She said "Thank you" and told me to sit down
and read a magazine and have a cup of coffee . . .
and wait for my name to be called.

He sees many things, but does not observe them;
his ears are open, but he does not hear. . . .
Who among you will give ear to this,
will attend and listen for the time to come?
Isaiah 42:20, 23

*Enable us, O God, to learn how to be content in whatever
state we are in, and may our minds be ever calmed by
our trust in you.*

ALONE IN THE WAITING ROOM

Here I sit, God, waiting for some news—
    a definite word, an inkling of hope,
    just something to break the tension
    and terror of this moment.

I look around in desperation, God—
    maybe misery does love company, after all—
    and I see the other people waiting with me.
There is a young couple sitting in the corner;
    I think I saw them come in with their baby.
There's an older woman across the aisle,
    her eyes red and puffy, perhaps from crying.
There's a man about my age, drinking coffee,
    who just sits and stares at the floor.
We are all here, Lord, waiting for something,
    for news of what's going on behind closed doors.

But even as I look at these people in waiting,
    I feel so terribly alone.
This is all so stark and sudden.
I don't know what to think or what to wait for.

Lord, the words of a song I learned
    in camp as a boy just flashed through my mind.
It was called "Kum Ba Yah."
Doesn't it mean to come by here?

Will you come by here then, Lord,
    and wait with me?

So then you are no longer strangers and sojourners, but
you are fellow citizens with the saints and members of
the household of God.

Ephesians 2:19

Help us, O God, to understand that we are all alike in our suffering and our need for your redemptive love. Come to each of us so that we all may know that we are never alone and may always find a home with you.

IT CAN'T BE HER; IT CAN'T BE ME

I'll never forget that moment, God.
A tall young resident walked into the waiting room
    of the hospital.
"Your wife has had a massive stroke," he said.
"It's probably fatal; she's slipped into a coma
    and probably won't live out the day."

Later on they said it was worse than they thought,
    and I should go right home and get the children.
They needed to come say goodbye to their mother.

God, this can't be real.
It can't be her, it can't be me.
We were just together, and now she's going to die?

I've always looked at things for what they are,
    but this is absurd. I can't believe it!
I've got to have her get up and come home now.
I need her, God.
There's hot coffee brewing on the stove,
    and we have a life to live.

Then his wife said to him, "Do you still hold fast your
integrity? Curse God, and die." But [Job] said to her,
"You speak as one of the foolish women would speak.
Shall we receive good at the hand of God, and shall we
not receive evil?"

Job 2:9–10

*Lord, help us to accept the reality that your ways are not
our ways, and lead us toward understanding and accept-
ing your will for our lives.*

SEVEN SIGNS

I started to read this pamphlet, God,
 "Seven Hopeful Facts About Stroke."
I was excited and encouraged as I began to read it
 until I realized what it was.
It was a warning against the seven signs
 that indicate a stroke is coming.

It wasn't what I had in mind
 when I picked it up.
It wasn't very helpful or hopeful—
 after the fact.

The fact is, God, he's had a stroke
 whether either of us heeded the warning signs
 or not.
The fact is, half of my husband
 doesn't work anymore.

And here I sit by his bedside,
 looking for signs of hope,
 wondering what the truth is about his condition
 and what the outcome will be.

I look back at that pamphlet
 in my mind's eye, God,
 wishing it would tell me something,
 wishing it would live up to its name.

And God said, "This is the sign of the covenant which
I make between me and you and every living creature
that is with you, for all future generations."

Genesis 9:12

Lord God, we call you by name looking for signs of hope. Give us the patience and encouragement in our despairing moments to face change and overcome our fears.

TELLING THE CHILDREN

God, this is a nightmare.
I stumbled out of the hospital
    after hearing the news.
I don't remember driving home,
    just the faces of the children
    when I walked through the door.
They had a look of terror, shock, and unbelief
    as I led them into the family room.

We all sat down and I began to tell them
    as calmly and simply as I could:
    Mom has had a very bad stroke.
    Her head is full of blood.
    I don't think she will be with us very long.
    We all need to go and see her to say goodbye.

"No!" my daughter screamed at me, as she
    ran out the door and down the street,
    as if running away from the news
    would make it go away.
"Come back!" yelled our older son and ran after her,
    as if he needed her to face the truth with him.
Our younger son sat slumped forward in his chair,
    his head in his hands, crying.
I watched his tears dropping onto the floor.

Now I am in our bedroom, Lord, alone,
    pounding my fists on the bed
    in which she nearly died,
    screaming and cursing at you.
God, what has happened here?
    What have you done?
    What has she done?
    What have we done to deserve this?

Blessed be the God and Father of our Lord Jesus Christ, the Father of mercies and God of all comfort, who comforts us in all our affliction, so that we may be able to comfort those who are in any affliction, with the comfort with which we ourselves are comforted by God.

                                        2 Corinthians 1:3–4

Lord, even when we feel empty and estranged from you, help us to give our all to others so that they may know your peace and love, for in that way, God, we shall be filled with your Spirit.

AT HOME WITH MY THOUGHTS

It's over, Lord, the first day.
There was nothing I could do for him
    at the hospital.
They told me his condition was stable
    and I should go home and get some rest.
My cynical side always thought that meant:
    "Please leave now,
    you've been in the way long enough."
I did what they asked, God, and left.
I guess he's in good hands there.
The trouble is they're not mine.

I look around the house, Lord,
    and realize how big it is for the two of us,
    let alone one.
He's there and I'm here—
    it was such a brutally quick separation.
Please don't make it long
    and please don't make it permanent.
I'm just not ready to give him up.

They say the first forty-eight hours
    are the most critical, God.
So far it's only been twelve.
Twelve down and thirty-six to go
    and counting.

God, are they serious?
How can they expect me to rest
    at a time like this?
When at any minute I could get a call:
    "I'm sorry, but there's been a change
    in your husband's condition—
    you'd better come back here right away."

Lord, please keep the phone from ringing tonight,
   and maybe I can get some rest.
Lord, stay with me tonight;
   I've never been this alone before.

In peace I will both lie down and sleep;
   for thou alone, O LORD, makest me dwell in
      safety.

                                        Psalm 4:8

*Thank you, Lord, for your presence. May we always be
aware of your calm and peace and that you are forever
with us to protect, forgive, and lead us home.*

TWO

ACCEPTING THE FACTS

COMING TO TERMS WITH REALITY

I've always believed, Lord,
   that if you face the truth
   you never need to be afraid.
The truth is, I don't know what I am facing here,
   and I am very much afraid.

As I walked into the main entrance of the hospital
   it began to hit me all over again.
With every step upstairs and down the hall
   my apprehension grows.

As I stand at the doorway and peek into his room
   I hesitate to go in.
I'm afraid of what I will see: him lying there,
   behind the bars of his hospital bed,
   helpless and disheveled, attached to all the
   tubes and machines that monitor his condition.

As I walk to his side, Lord,
   I begin to imagine that I will awaken him
   and he will open his eyes and look at me
   and then he will yawn and stretch
   and then he will climb out of bed
   and ask me why I let him oversleep
   and what I made for breakfast.
Maybe he will even recall we were supposed to have
   breakfast at church today with our friends.

A nurse comes in behind me, God;
   her very presence brings me back to reality.
She tells me he's passed a quiet night,
   that his vital signs are normal
   and the doctor will be in to see me soon.

She takes his pulse and leaves the room,
    telling me he's had quite a shock to his system
    and he'll be a long time getting better.

I've had quite a shock to my system too, Lord,
    and I know I can't escape its effects.
But with your help, I can begin even now
    to accept the enormity of our situation
    and I can begin to make it better—
    for both of us.

And Peter said to him, "Aeneas, Jesus Christ heals you;
rise and make your bed." And immediately he rose.

Acts 9:34

*Lord God, we know that you have the power to heal and
that you seek to share it with us. Help us to face up to
our broken lives and receive your healing as you intend
for us to have it.*

LAMENTING THE PAST

God, I should have known! The headaches—
I remember the one last fall;
    she fell on her knees and held her head
    and banged it on the floor.
I remember her saying,
    "This really is a bad one, honey."
I held her so tightly, Lord,
    trying to squeeze the pain out of her.
Finally she took the pills,
    two extra ones this time,
    and the headache went away.
Why didn't I insist we get help?
The pills always did the trick before, God.
I was afraid of the headaches
    and wanted to forget them.
The pills helped me to do that.

But why didn't I do something else?
Why didn't I insist on getting help
    instead of being such a coward
    and playing so fast and loose with her life?
If only I had acted on my best intentions, God,
    instead of my worst fears.
If only. . . . Lord, I wonder.
I wonder how many expressions of past regret
    begin with those words, "If only"?
They are so often said in despair and helplessness
    while we watch our worst fears come true.

For the Lord will not
    cast off for ever,
but, though he cause grief, he will have compassion

according to the abundance of his steadfast love;
for he does not willingly afflict
or grieve the sons of men.

                                        Lamentations 3:31–33

*Almighty God, as you came to those long ago with assur-
ances of your tender love and care, may we trust in you
today to lift us up and deliver us from our fears and
afflictions. May your promise of peace come true again
for us.*

KEEPING WATCH

She's made it through the weekend, Lord,
    against all odds and medical advice.
It's a new week, a new day,
    and time has become very precious.

We keep watch over her, God,
    looking for signs that she's improved.
Her heartbeat has stabilized;
    they may try to take her off the respirator
    to see if she can breathe on her own.

This morning she grimaced and raised her arm;
    she seemed to be stretching
    and about to wake up from a deep sleep.
I'm suddenly encouraged, God,
    but the nurses say these are all reflex actions
    and that she really didn't make them happen.

The children and some of our friends
    are taking shifts to be with her.
They have decided to "coach" her back to health.
They tell her to do things
    to show that she's still with us:
    "Wiggle your toes, move your arm again,
    make a face, open your eyes . . .
    wake up now."

No response. But she's beaten the odds so far
    and we'll keep on trying if she will.
She's worth the effort, Lord.
She's needed. She's loved.

But as for me, I will look to the LORD,
  I will wait for the God of my salvation;
  my God will hear me.

Micah 7:7

*Dear God, help us to use the hours of our life to develop
the courage and patience to wait faithfully for you and
receive your blessing and peace.*

APRAXIA, APHASIA, HEMIPLEGIA?

I look at my husband and he looks back at me.
I see in his eyes that he wants to speak to me,
   but he can't.
The nurses call this aphasia—or is it apraxia?

I can't remember, Lord.
All these medical terms are so new to me.
Everything is so strange here in the hospital.
I'm so confused and afraid.
I've lost control of my life.
He and I have always been able to help each other.
Now there's nothing I can do for him.

The doctors told me all I can do is wait,
   and hope, and pray.
I can pray, but how can I just sit by and wait?
When it hurts so much?
When I feel so helpless?
What can I do, God?
What will happen—to him, to me, to us?

For now we see in a mirror dimly, but then face to face.
Now I know in part; then I shall understand fully, even
as I have been fully understood. So faith, hope, love
abide, these three; but the greatest of these is love.
1 Corinthians 13:12–13

*Lord, we know that somewhere in the future our trials
and tribulations will make sense to us. Help us to wait
patiently for that time while we live through these days.*

PRIVATE INVESTIGATING

Lord, I've read through every book I could find
   about strokes.
I know more than I really understand.
I know more than I want to know
   about what happened to him.
I even wrote down all the questions
   I could think of, to ask his doctor.
We talked for two hours, God.

A stroke is an interruption of the flow of blood
   to a certain part of the brain.
My husband had a stroke in the left hemisphere.
He's paralyzed on the right side, and he has lost
   his power of speech.
It's going to take a lot of work,
But we can expect some of the paralysis to go
   and a lot of his speech to return.

Now that I know the diagnosis and the prognosis,
   I feel less afraid.
But I still don't know if I can deal with this;
   it's been so sudden and overwhelming.
I spoke with my pastor, too, about this stroke.
He said I could face up to it
   and help my husband overcome the deficits,
   but not without your help, God.

O God, help me.
Help me look into myself now.
Give me those hidden strengths to confront and
   confound whatever malevolent power brought
   this stroke into our lives.
Give me the patience to wait
   for a meaningful ending to all this suffering.

Help me to help him, God.
And give me credit for trying to understand and
  accept all of what has happened to us.

But they who wait for the LORD shall renew their
    strength,
  they shall mount up with wings like eagles,
they shall run and not be weary,
  they shall walk and not faint.

Isaiah 40:31

*Dear Redeemer God, reveal your truth to us in your time,
and then we will be truly free.*

A HEART-TO-HEART WITH A FRIEND

It's been more than a week now, Lord;
   the only news is bad;
   and the only signals point
   to things getting progressively worse.

There's no improvement, no signs of life.
Her doctors decided she needed a tracheostomy;
   she just can't breathe on her own.
They have also reported pneumonia in both lungs,
   and the infection is spreading through her body.

A dear friend of ours called this morning, God.
She wanted to know how things were going.
I told her and she cried over the phone
   and asked me to meet her for lunch.

We ate and drank—maybe more than I should have.
I talked and she listened.
She talked and I listened,
   perhaps just as I should have a week or so ago
   when the doctors told me not to get my hopes up.
She said that each of us is in your care, God,
   and even though my wife is very sick
   her life is still precious in your sight.
She told me to lean on her and trust in you,
   and I would come to see a way out of my sorrow.

Lord, I know that you keep us all
   folded within your everlasting arms.
So do hold her ever so gently
   and help me to do the same.

Besides my own, God,
   hers is the only life I know
   and I love her as I do myself.

And in my better moments, God,
  when I come to think about it,
  I love her even more.

We are afflicted in every way, but not crushed; per-
plexed, but not driven to despair; persecuted, but not
forsaken; struck down, but not destroyed.

2 Corinthians 4:8–9

Thank you, God, for your words of assurance that come
from those we know and love, who provide us with the
strength to face the challenges of this day and the days
that lie ahead.

BARELY HOLDING ON

Damn it all, God!
I've had it!
I can't take it anymore.
What did I do to earn this?
Why did he leave me like this?
Why did you make this happen?

I always believed, God,
    because I was always taught to believe,
    that you would take care of us
    and he would take care of me.
That's why I believed in you, God,
    and why I married him.

Now you have both let me down!
Everything has changed.
He's taken care of now;
    he's fed and toileted
    and lifted from his bed to his chair.
And you, God—
You seem absent and removed from all of this.
You've done your worst
    and left the scene of the accident.
I don't know where to go from here.
I don't know what to believe or whom to trust.
I'm at the end of my tether
    and just barely holding on.

The LORD is good,
    a stronghold in the day of trouble;
    he knows those who take refuge in him.
                                    Nahum 1:7

Help us, O Lord, to trust in you this day. Be our refuge and strength and hold us close to you in times of danger and distress.

MAKING EXPLANATIONS

This is not going to be an easy day for me, God.

Yesterday was bad enough.
I had to call our daughter to update her
    on how her father was.
They've always been so close, Lord.
When she was growing up
    she thought he was invincible;
    he thought she was perfect.
Now that he's sick and she's so far away
    she feels lost and helpless because
    there's nothing she can do.

I tell her not to worry,
    and I hear the apprehension in her voice.
I want to do something for her
    just as she does for him.
But I realize there is nothing
    that either of us can do—
    except to wait and pray.
But right now, God, that doesn't seem to be enough.

Today I must go and see his mother.
She's gotten so forgetful lately.
I've had to tell her twice he's had a stroke,
    and she cried the second time
    just as much as she did at first.
I hate to hurt her feelings;
    she's always so glad to see me
    when I come by the house.
Will I have to tell her all over again today?
I'm afraid to find out.

I don't even want to show up, God.
I'm so tired of being the bearer
    of bad news.
I'm tired of hearing it, of telling it;
I'm tired of making explanations and excuses
    for things I don't understand that aren't my fault.

But, for whatever reason,
    I know I'm the one who has to hold on here.
Please help me then to accept this,
    my present lot in life.
Help me to make it through this day
    and all the days after this one
    as well as I am able,
    as well as you desire.

I can do all things in him who strengthens me.
                                        Philippians 4:13

*Give me strength, God, to keep holding on, and help me
to share it with those who depend upon me.*

MISLEADING LABELS

Lord, I'll be forever trying to sort this out,
    it's all so hard to comprehend.
Just as I was beginning to understand
    what the effects of a left-side stroke were,
    as opposed to the effects of a right-sided one,
I heard a nurse talking about red strokes
    and green strokes.

All these terms seem silly to me, God.
Do strokes come in colors?
Can we choose what direction they come from?
Does a red stroke mean you stay as you are
    and a green one mean you go on and get better?

I feel so dumb, God,
    as if everyone knows what I don't know
    and they want to keep it from me.
I'm a foreigner here; I don't speak the language.
I feel out of place when I come in.
This must be something of what my husband feels,
    and he's here all the time.

Please, Lord, as long as we are here
    help us to feel welcome and at home.

By the waters of Babylon, there we sat down and
        wept,
    when we remembered Zion. . . .
How shall we sing the LORD's song in a foreign
        land?

                              Psalm 137:1, 4

Lord, help us to realize that we are never strangers to you, and even in the midst of our doubts and confusion you will always guide and protect us.

FRIENDS IN THE CHURCH

There's a column in our church newsletter, God,
  called the "Intercessor."
It lists all the people in our congregation
  who are ill and shut in,
  who need a prayer or a phone call,
  a get-well card or a home visit.

This week my husband's name was on the list.
We've received cards and flowers from more people
  than we even know at church.
Plus we've gotten several phone calls
  and visits at home and in the hospital.

I never gave it a second thought
  when I sent cards to others when they were sick.
Now I know just how good it feels
  to be remembered by people who really care.

My sewing circle sent a little book of devotions.
I read through it, Lord, and was reminded
  that you care too.
The words of comfort and assurance
  made me realize how much a part
  of our lives you really are.

Sometimes, God, I do get angry at you, at him,
  the doctors, and anyone else who may be in the way.
But when I have a moment to pause and reflect
  on the kindness of friends and your tender mercies,
  I realize what it is to be loved for who we are
  and I feel special and very grateful.

Bear one another's burdens, and so fulfil the law of Christ.

Galatians 6:2

Help us, O Lord, to follow your law and to rejoice in serving others.

A VISIT WITH THE THERAPIST

Every day she comes into the room, God.
She takes my wife's hands in her own
    and massages them.
She moves her wrists and bends her elbows;
    she raises her legs and bends her knees.

I came in early one morning and saw her at work.
She said the human body wasn't made to lie dormant.
It was made to move.
And if my wife couldn't move her body on her own,
    then she would do it for her.
That was what she did as a physical therapist.

I watched and spoke with her while she worked, God.
She said she didn't want my wife to wake up
    with foot drop or contractures.
I thought how noble a gesture this was;
    such a simple act of devotion and hope
    in the midst of so much confusion and despair.
It wasn't *if* she woke up, God, but *when*.
Does she know something no one else does?
Did the therapist feel something, Lord,
    in her muscles or her bones,
    some life-giving impulse that would cause my wife
    to open her eyes?

Lord, is there some secret to all this,
    something of your will and nature
    that I have yet to see?

Keep your heart with all vigilance;
    for from it flow the springs of life.
                                    Proverbs 4:23

Lord, so often you reveal yourself to us in such quiet and simple ways that we overlook them. As we wait and wonder, God, show us how your strength is sown in our weakness and your love revealed in the kindnesses of others.

THREE

LIVING
WITH THE EFFECTS
OF STROKE

COPING

Lord, today is Sunday. I went to church alone
    for the first time since he got sick.
I know I should be able to worship by myself;
    but we've always done it together as a couple.
It was so lonely and painful being there without him.
Friends kept asking over and over,
    "How is he?"
    "What do the doctors say?"

After church I went to the hospital to see him.
I told him about the service and how everyone
    asked after him.
I tried to make it sound exciting
    but he saw right through me.
First he gave a crooked smile, and then he cried,
    and then he mumbled that he wanted to come home
    and go to church with me.

O Lord, I want him to come home too.
But I want him whole and complete.
Is that too much to ask or expect?
It's been three weeks now, and he still can't talk
    or speak clearly or do things for himself.
I'm in so much conflict here, God.
I want my husband back the way he was—
    even with all his faults.
And yet I don't know how to accept him as he is
    or the fact that he may always be this way.

God, help me to cope with all these feelings.
Help me to separate him from his illness.
Help me to love and accept him just as he is;
    just as he has always done for me.

I lift up my eyes to the hills.
From whence does my help come?
My help comes from the LORD,
    who made heaven and earth.
                        Psalm 121:1–2

*Almighty God, help us to look up and realize that you
are strong to save and eager to satisfy us with your steadfast love.*

PAYING OUR FAIR SHARE

Lord, I've been so upset
  I forgot to talk to the insurance company.
I finally called them to see what they would pay.
They spoke about co-payments and deductibles,
  and told me to contact Medicare,
  who spoke about the same things.

Lord, all these days in Intensive Care,
  all the doctors who came in to examine him,
  they look at him, and then at me,
  and then mumble a polite word and leave.
Yesterday I received a bill
  from doctors I never heard of.
I wonder what they did for him?

God, I am so worried about this!
I know I have to pay, but how much?
Will we lose all our savings to this stroke,
  everything we have worked for?
The illness is bad enough, God,
  but this is just not fair.

Have no anxiety about anything, but in everything by
prayer and supplication with thanksgiving let your re-
quests be made known to God. And the peace of God,
which passes all understanding, will keep your hearts
and your minds in Christ Jesus.

Philippians 4:6–7

*We thank you, God, for the assurance that you hear our
prayers and you grant us your peace. Cast out our fears
and keep us ever in your mind and care.*

TALKING WITH THE SECURITY GUARD

Each night I walk by the security guard, Lord,
    when I go up to her room.
I've noticed that they change shifts a lot,
    but there's one guard I've come to recognize,
    and he seems to know me too.

I said hello one night as I passed him in the hall.
He returned the greeting and then asked,
    "How's your wife?"
"Not very well," I replied, forcing half a smile.
"I was working the day she came in," he said;
    "it looked pretty bad. I'm sorry she's sick;
    she's a very pretty lady."
I thanked him, and with a small but grateful tear
    continued down the hall and up the stairs
    to see her, my very pretty lady.

The pain and despair is always with me, God,
    but the burden is always lifted
    when I meet someone who cares.
I thank you for acknowledgment and support
    that come from unexpected places.
I can sure use it, Lord; I relish it.
I hope it comes again.

For just as the body is one and has many members, and
all the members of the body, though many, are one
body, so it is with Christ.

                                    1 Corinthians 12:12

*Lord, help me to live in fellowship with you, as I also find
the reality of your presence in the lives of those around
me.*

BEING A MANAGEMENT PROBLEM

Before I went into his room today, God,
    a young nurse stopped me in the hall
    and asked if we could have a conference.
A conference? Why not just "a word or two,"
    or "Could I speak with you for a moment?"

We went into a small room
    where I assumed conferences like this were held,
    and we sat down at a table.
The nurse looked at me and began.
    "Your husband is becoming a management problem
    and we don't know how to handle him."
I looked back in surprise and asked
    what a management problem was
    and how my husband came to be one.
She said he wouldn't eat or take his medicine
    and struck out at one of the other nurses
    on the midnight shift last night.
She and the other members of the staff
    would appreciate my help
    in making him a little more cooperative.

I didn't know what to think, Lord.
I felt like saying it was their problem
    and their job to take care of him—
    that's why he was in the hospital.
But I thought again and held my tongue.
I know they're doing the best they can here;
    I know they're shorthanded and overworked
    and by asking me to help them
    they are only trying to help him.

But you understand, Lord.
I've never before been asked
   to help "manage" my husband.
I've just wanted to care for him—
   at home, in the hospital, or wherever.
He's always managed by himself.

Lord, help me to manage by myself.
Help me to be willing and cooperative and helpful
   so that we can make him well again.

For they gave according to their means, as I can testify,
and beyond their means, of their own free will, begging
us earnestly for the favor of taking part in the relief of
the saints.

                                        2 Corinthians 8:3–4

*Lord, always keep us ready and willing to give our care
to those who need it.*

PATIENT RIGHTS

I wondered to myself, Lord,
    What makes him behave like this?
He's never been that way at home.
He's getting the best of care in the hospital
    from people who care about him.
Why is he being so difficult?

I talked to our children about him.
Our son put his finger right on it.
"Dad has a right to act that way.
None of us can imagine what a stroke is like
    or how frustrated and afraid he must be. . . .
I think he's dealing with it as best he can."

He has a right, God.
We all need to understand that
    while we're watching over him.

I remember seeing "The Patient's Bill of Rights"
    on the wall in the hospital corridor.
Maybe I should add one more to the list.
"A patient has the right to let caregivers know
    whenever he feels angry and afraid—
    even if it makes caregivers feel the same way."

It isn't easy, God, managing my husband's illness.
But help us all to remember, myself especially,
    that it's a lot more difficult for him,
    and we who are well have an obligation
    to ease his pain.

Let each of you look not only to his own interests, but
also to the interests of others.

Philippians 2:4

Lord, help us to overlook what is comfortable and seems right to us to understand the pain of others and involve ourselves in their suffering.

COACHING SESSIONS

I've been meeting twice a week with her doctor
   for some time now, God.
They have become coaching sessions, in a way.

At first he just gave me news of her condition—
   breathing difficulties, spread of infection—
   and I would try to absorb what he was saying.
But then, as her condition began to stabilize,
   I was able to process more of his information,
   and I began to ask questions,
   and he began to answer.
I wanted to understand
   as much about this tragedy as possible.
I had to learn.
I think he realized that
   and respected my right to know.

We began to talk to each other, God,
   not just as physician and husband
   but as newfound acquaintances
   and then as friends, sharing a common concern
   over someone he cared about
   and I loved deeply.

He began to sense my feelings,
   and often his attention would turn
   from her condition to my own.
"Get rest," he said. "Keep order in your life,
   and don't come in so much.
I'll call you if anything happens."

I listened to his advice, God;
   it felt good to be cared for,
   although there is one thing
   I just can't do.

I can't stay away; I've got to be with her
  whenever I can.

So I didn't take all his advice, Lord.
But I remember playing ball in college—
  I never followed the coach's orders
  all the time then, either.

Therefore encourage one another and build one another
up, just as you are doing.

                                   1 Thessalonians 5:11

*God of help and deliverance, we thank you for those who
follow your examples and help us. Now let us follow their
way as we give help to others.*

NURSING CARE

Nurses are special people, Lord.
Their title almost guarantees
    the quality of their work.
To nurse is to nurture, protect, to give care.
Each time I watch the nurses work with her,
    bathing her, turning her, changing her gown,
    putting an extra pillow behind her head,
    I see their dedication unfolding
    in living color right before my eyes.

They talk to her as if she really hears them,
    and they believe she does.
They comb her hair each morning
    and pull down the window shade
    when the sun shines too brightly on her face.
One of them even put a little rouge on her cheeks
    and dabbed some perfume behind her ear
    before she let me in to visit.

I doubt that any of them learned
    to do these things in nursing school, Lord.
It comes naturally, and people who become nurses
    are people who care for others long before
    they are taught or told to care.

It's really not something you can learn—
    nursing, protecting, caring.
It's a gift that comes from you, Lord.
And I want you to know
    that my wife's nurses use their gifts very well.

Practice hospitality ungrudgingly to one another. As each has received a gift, employ it for one another, as good stewards of God's varied grace.

1 Peter 4:9–10

We are all created in your image, God. Thank you for those who live up to it in their care and devotion to the needs of others.

THE WHOOSH OF THE RESPIRATOR

The instant I enter the ICU, Lord,
  it makes its ominous welcome.
I can close my eyes and hear it everywhere—
  the whoosh of the respirator.
She's had three different ones already,
  but they're all alike and do the same thing.
They breathe for her as she sleeps.
Not the way she does, soft and sweet,
  but rather with a loud rushing nasal sound,
  as air is forced through the bellows
  of the machine and then into her lungs.

Again and again I hear it, Lord,
  until it becomes part of our life together.
She can't live without it, nor I without her,
  so I share her with the respirator
  in a not-so-peaceful coexistence.
I do resent this noisy mechanical wonder
  that's become such a critical part of our lives.
It constantly tells me how fragile and fleeting
  the notions of our independence are
  and how much we want to be free.

I feel the same way about you sometimes, God.
I want to be free from you and go where I please.
I grow weary from the constant pressure
  of knowing you are part of my life.
It makes me feel I am always having
  to please you instead.
But her illness and my pain remind me, God,
  of how close you are to me in a different way.
There is no pressure on your part
  to be entertained or appeased,
  just this gentle prodding of my consciousness

to make me more aware of your yearning and desire
to bring a calming peace into my life
and the wonder of your constant love.

Whither shall I go from thy Spirit?
    Or whither shall I flee from thy presence?
If I ascend to heaven, thou art there!
    If I make my bed in Sheol, thou are there!
If I take the wings of the morning
    and dwell in the uttermost parts of the sea,
even there thy hand shall lead me,
    and thy right hand shall hold me.

                                        Psalm 139:7–10

Lord, when we are casting about in turmoil and confu-
sion, bring our restless souls home to be at peace with
you.

INSERTING THE TRACHEOSTOMY TUBE

Her doctor gave me news today, Lord.
Her breathing tube needs to be removed
    because breathing through her mouth
    will eventually ruin her vocal cords.
If she ever wakes up, she won't be able to talk.
For now, though, there's no choice but to advise
    a tracheostomy.
He'd like me to sign a consent form.

The doctor explained all this before, Lord;
    I knew it was coming.
But the idea that she is breathing
    on a machine and now with a hole in her throat
    borders on the unbearable for me.
"It really will be better," he said.
"Her mouth won't be distorted by tubes anymore,
    and we can regulate her breathing more easily."

I understand, God, that it's for the best.
But it all feels so permanent to me,
    like we're admitting failure
    and taking a major step backward.
Sound the retreat. My wife, by virtue of the best
    professional medical advice I can find,
    must be surgically attached to a machine to live.

Is this living, God?
Is this life as you created it?
Is this the life she would have wanted?
Or are we re-creating life—the quality of which
    is unacceptable to all of us?

Husbands, love your wives, as Christ loved the church and gave himself up for her.

Ephesians 5:25

Lord, be with us in a special way when we must watch the suffering of those whom we love as much as you love us. Help us to suffer with them as you do with us until their suffering ends.

BECOME A LEGAL GUARDIAN

Time does move on, Lord.
Even in the midst of crisis there is always
    the business of life to contend with.

My attorney called this morning
    with some professional advice of his own.
Since we had no power of attorney between us,
    I need to be legal guardian of my wife's affairs.
It will require an investigation of all parties,
    and a court hearing before a judge,
    and substantial legal fees.
And it has to be done, he said,
    or I could lose control of everything—
    even our home.

So we began the process, God,
    aimed at determining whether I was a
    suitable candidate to be her legal guardian.
The attorneys, one for her and one for me,
    started asking questions.
They asked questions of me; they asked questions
    about me and questions around me.
They spoke to the children, the rest
    of the family, and selected friends.
For three days I was the center of attention,
    the sole object of their curiosity.

Finally the research was completed and compiled
    and we went before the judge with our petition.
He looked it over in the space of five minutes,
    and with the signing of the decree
    I became the legal guardian for my wife.
I can now spend our money and keep our house
    and make all decisions I need to on her behalf.

Lord, this was a privilege I never sought
    or even believed I would obtain.
I am an ordinary man,
    and all I ever wanted
    was to be her loving husband
    and she my loving wife.
And now it has come to this.
How did all of this happen, God?
How did things get this far?

If you really fulfil the royal law, according to the scripture, "You shall love your neighbor as yourself," you
do well.

James 2:8

*Help us to understand, God, that so much of what we do
in life affects the welfare of others. Give us patience, then,
to contend with the necessary affairs of life—even when
we are beset by crisis.*

WHO'S IN CHARGE HERE?

Even in the midst of critical illness life goes on.
I used to watch when he did our taxes
　　or filled out loan applications.
He always checked himself as "Head of Household."
Now, it seems, that title has been passed on to me.

You know I didn't ask for it, God, and I'm not sure
　　what the job requires.
I see the bills are due, but his last pay check
　　hasn't arrived yet.
I know the roof has a leak, but I don't know
　　who to call to fix it.
I notice the grass needs cutting but I can't
　　push the mower by myself.
I don't like this newly earned status, God—
　　I don't deserve it.

I pray that this change in management
　　is only temporary.
But I wonder how long I have to live with this—
　　the decisions, the pressure and anguish.
When does the burden of responsibility revert back
　　to its rightful owner?
When can he resume his rightful place
　　as "Head of Household"?

Cast all your anxieties on him, for he cares about you.
. . . And after you have suffered a little while, the God

of all grace, who has called you to his eternal glory in Christ, will himself restore, establish, and strengthen you.

1 Peter 5:7, 10

Ever-constant God, let our prayers for peace reach out to all who must suffer from the effects of change.

PHYSICALLY HANDICAPPED, PHYSICALLY CHALLENGED

I watched while he went through his routine
   with the physical therapists.
They helped him lie down on the mat
   and asked him to move his leg.
He tried, and he couldn't.
They helped him sit up
   to see if he could raise his arm.
He tried, and he could, a little.

As I thanked you for these small victories, God,
   I noticed a pamphlet on the table called
   "Exercise Tips for the Physically Challenged."
I like the sound of that.
I'm glad there was no reference
   to the "physically handicapped."
Being handicapped sounds
   like a permanent condition,
   the kind where you're never expected to improve,
   and you get special license plates
   and put your car in special parking spaces
   right in front of mall entrances.

Being physically challenged, though,
   is a different thing altogether.
Being physically challenged is to be invigorated;
   it's something to live up to and aspire to,
   a goal to meet, an obstacle to overcome.

Lord, as I see him facing the physical obstacles
   of his illness,
   I hope he sees himself as challenged
   and not handicapped.
And by your spirit may he discover in himself

the stamina and motivation he needs to recover
his ability to walk again.
Then he won't be suffering
from the effects of a handicap, God.
He'll exceed our expectations of his progress
and surprise us all.
Then we won't need special parking at the mall.
We'll walk all the way there together.

In thy strength the king rejoices, O LORD;
and in thy help how greatly he exults!
Thou hast given him his heart's desire,
and hast not withheld the request of his lips.
Psalm 21:1–2

*Lord, each day brings new tasks and responsibilities.
Help us to recall that we are never equal to these challenges except by your strength and inspiration.*

ALL IN A DAY'S WORK

Before I finally get to the hospital today, Lord,
  I've got to get my hair done;
  I've got to go to the bank, the post office,
  and the dry cleaners, attend a meeting at church,
  and drop off a birthday cake for our grandson.
After I leave the hospital,
  I can rush over to our son's house just in time
  to watch our grandson blow the candles out.

Lord, you give us only so many hours in a day.
I can't seem to get it all done in one day anymore
  and there's more to do tomorrow.
Tomorrow? Don't I have a dentist appointment?
And doesn't my sewing group meet tomorrow night?
When will I have time to sit down
  and try to make some sense out of
  all the medical bills we have received?
I've lost track of who owes what to whom.

God, I am tired—in body, mind, and soul.
There is so much to do.
People ask if they can help.
And even if they're just being polite
  I wish I could say yes and get some relief
  from all my responsibilities.
But there are things I have to do
  that nobody else can do—
  no one, that is, except you, Lord.
You can help me.
You can get me through the day
  because you know what my true needs are.
You can guide me through my thoughts and actions
  and help me to do the things I must do
  and discard the things I can't.

God, help me to use my time wisely.
Help me not to get carried away with details
    or overlook anything that's really important
    or anyone who really matters.
Give me the time to do the things that count,
    but let me take it a little more slowly.

But I trust in thee, O LORD,
    I say, "Thou art my God."
My times are in thy hand.
                    Psalm 31:14–15a

*Lord, help us to do the things we should and not do the
things we shouldn't and have the wisdom to know the
difference between the two.*

SEEING JIM ON THE STREET

It was an early Sunday morning, God,
  a cold gray one at that.
I was walking to church after a moment with her,
  and I saw Jim walking toward me.
His eyes lit up when he saw me; it had been awhile.
He came up quickly and shook my hand
  and asked after me and where she was.
Jim has an antique store near our home.
He always adored her when we went in to browse.

I told Jim I was on my way to church,
  and then I paused
  and said she was in the hospital,
  dying from a stroke.
Jim fell back, aghast, and his eyes began to fill.
He protested that she was too young and beautiful
  and it couldn't be true.
I just stood and looked at him through my own tears
  to let the truth sink in.
Finally, Lord, we embraced and cried together,
  two men on a city street on a cold gray Sunday,
  and I asked him to pray for her
  while I went off to church.

Lord, her life touched the lives of many others,
  like Jim, before her stroke.
Is it really going to end now?
Will she never touch another life
  such as Jim's, or mine, again?

Out of my distress I called on the LORD;
  the LORD answered me and set me free. . . .

This is the day which the LORD has made.
                              Psalm 118:5, 24

*When fear surrounds us, Lord, come and encircle us
with the gentle power of your redeeming love and let us
rejoice and be glad in it.*

LOSING GROUND TO PNEUMONIA

God, I had another chat with her doctor today.
I could see the anguish on his face,
and I knew there was nothing good to tell.
Her pneumonia is getting worse,
the infection is spreading, and it's beginning
to affect her kidney and liver functions.

It's such an insidious thing, God, this pneumonia.
Her stroke was the worst shock of my life,
but at least it was obvious in its effect.
It didn't sneak around her body
slowly destroying one part after another,
draining her life away.
The antibiotics are no longer doing their job.
There's a battle going on inside her
that no one can fight for her
and she can't win by herself.
The truth is that things are looking worse each day.
I've always asked for the truth, God,
but the truth is now
that I don't want to hear it anymore.

This is no way to live,
not for a moment or a day—
not for her or any of us.
Lord, do something now, please.
Make your will be done.

But he said to her, "You speak as one of the foolish
women would speak. Shall we receive good at the hand
of God, and shall we not receive evil?"

Job 2:10

Lord, in desperate times we are called to take bold action. Let us then never be anxious but thank you for our adversity, that we may come to understand true peace and deliverance.

FORTY DAYS AND FORTY NIGHTS

Lord, it seems a short time since it happened,
And yet it also seems so long.
The days run together as I keep my vigil over her,
And then I realize that in the last forty days
   almost everyone in the hospital learned my name.

I go to see her in the ICU every night.
I pull down the shades in her room
   and sit on the edge of her bed.
I try to talk and pray with her amid the *whoosh*
   of the respirator that keeps her breathing.
I try to hold her amid all the tubes in her chest
   and in her arms that keep her alive.
I long for a response from her, Lord.
She sleeps; she doesn't wake; she doesn't move.
I long for a change for the better.
She takes a turn for the worse.

God, I feel so alone here,
   all my tears of sadness and despair.
I know more about strokes than I ever planned,
   but it seems so worthless to me now.

My soul thirsts for God,
   for the living God. . . .
My tears have been my food
   day and night,
while men say to me continually,
   "Where is your God?" . . .
Hope in God: for I shall again praise him,
   my help and my God.
                    Psalm 42:2, 3, 11

Lord, be with each of us in the dark nights of our souls, and then when your light breaks forth upon us let us rise up and give thanks for our deliverance.

HOW IS GOD REVEALED HERE?

God, her coma deepened, her pneumonia spread.
Yesterday she had an episode of cardiac arrest.
Her physician called me and asked ever so gently,
  "Would you consider moving her to a nursing home?
  There's really nothing else that we can do."

You are the Creator and Sustainer of all things.
I believe that, Lord.
But it is so hard for me to see
  how you are revealing yourself here.
Everything is so dark.
What are you doing here, God?
She is so far away from me.
I am so lost without her.
What has come between us?
What is the meaning of this?
What will you do now?

Look carefully then how you walk, not as unwise men
but as wise, making the most of the time, because the
days are evil. Therefore do not be foolish, but understand what the will of the Lord is.

Ephesians 5:15–17

*Lord, help us to discern your will for our lives and give
us wisdom to know that you also created the darkness
and we can find you even there.*

A FITTING RESPONSE

I've tried to avoid this decision for days now.
But I can't ignore the facts, Lord,
    or try to escape from reality any longer.
She is desperately ill, with virtually no chance
    of ever getting better.
She always said she never wanted to live this way.
I don't want her to live this way, God.
I don't believe you do either.
Yet her doctors say that she could go on like this
    for months or even years.

Lord, I know you are always at work in our lives.
You create all things and redeem them
    for your great purpose.
I must hold on to my faith here,
    but in good faith I must decide now to let her go.
You see, God, I want everything out of the way—
    physicians, nurses, machines, even myself—
    in order to see your redemptive work.
I love her too much to keep her any longer.
I give her up to you.
It's the fitting thing for me to do.

But, as it is written,
    "What no eye has seen, nor ear heard,
    nor the heart of man conceived,
    what God has prepared for those who love him,"
God has revealed to us.

1 Corinthians 2:9–10a

Lord, to whom shall we go when all seems lost for us? Thanks be to you for giving us the victory.

FOUR

ROAD
TO RECOVERY

"HELLO THERE"

I just had one of my twice-weekly talks with
    her doctor, Lord.
He noticed a further deterioration in her condition.
An old friend came to see her one last time.
We walked into her room together.
The warm spring sun shone through the window
    onto her face.
She seemed so peaceful lying there.
How could she be so close to death?
Our friend stood by the side of the bed,
    and held her hand in his own, and said, "Hello."

She opened her eyes and looked at me—and smiled!
She's awake!

"She's awake!" I shouted down the hall. *"Awake!"*
And soon her room was filled with nurses
    and physicians and aides and orderlies
    and people from all over the hospital.
There were tears of joy and looks of incredulity
    and cries of "Bravo!" as I kissed her
    and she kissed me back; as I asked her
    again and again, "Are you awake?"
    and she nodded her head: *yes . . . yes!*

This is your work, God.
This is a miracle!
I believe in miracles.
I saw one with my own eyes when she opened hers.

Jesus said to her, "Did I not tell you that if you would
believe you would see the glory of God?" . . . When he
had said this, he cried with a loud voice, "Lazarus,

come out." The dead man came out, his hands and feet bound with bandages, and his face wrapped with a cloth. Jesus said to them, "Unbind him, and let him go."

John 11:40, 43–44

Lord, thank you for those moments when you call us out of our misery into the splendid moment of your choosing when we can shout, "Hallelujah!"

GOING TO THERAPY

We began therapy this week, Lord.
This is real progress.
They used to come to her room
   and move her arms and legs
   to keep her limber and prevent contractures.
Now she goes to them.
Every morning she goes downstairs
   to the second floor of the hospital
   to meet her therapists for her daily routine.
She does sit-ups and leg bends on the exercise mat.
She walks between the parallel bars.
She works at remembering basic arithmetic.
She tries to recall the correct date and day
   of the week.
That may not seem like much to some people, Lord;
   but when you have come from lying down
   looking up at the bottom
   you have come a long way.

I'm so very proud of her, Lord.
She's so positive about herself,
   and she has this indomitable will to prevail.
Yesterday I went to get her after her session
   and found her waiting for me in her wheelchair
   in the hall by the window.
She was sitting very still, staring intently at a
   cardinal perched outside on the windowsill.
I stood there for a moment just to watch her.
To me she looked like a beautiful porcelain doll.
But then she noticed me; she looked up and smiled,
   and her green eyes sparkled as she exclaimed,
     "Hi, honey, I walked by myself today!"

Well, not quite, Lord, but close.
And I rejoice in the knowledge that the day will come.
Thank you, God.
Will your miracles never cease?

We rejoice in our hope of sharing the glory of God
. . . and hope does not disappoint us.

Romans 5:2, 5

Lord God, as we are so often forced to respond to the
painful demands of life, open our hearts to hear and to
know that you are always near.

"HONEY, I'M A FIGHTER"

Gradually, Lord, he's getting better.
I see improvement almost every day.
I went to his therapy session today and watched.
He walked, unassisted, between the parallel bars,
   one leg after the other, the good leg first,
   the other coming slowly from behind,
   until he reached the end.
After the session was over,
   I helped him back to his room.
He sat up in bed while I sat on the edge.
I kissed him and told him how well he was doing.
He looked at me proudly and said, as best he could,
   "Honey, I'm a fighter."

God, it's been so long since I felt this way—
   and since I've seen him feel the same—
   hopeful, proud, and confident of getting well.
Everyone says—doctors, nurses, therapists—
   that he will get better in time;
   it all depends on his attitude and frame of mind,
   as well as on my own.

But I'm not afraid the way I was before, God.
Deep in my heart I know he can do it.
He was always someone who got the job done,
   and I know he's still the man he was.
I'll just recall his words to me
   whenever I'm plagued by second thoughts:
   "Honey, I'm a fighter"!

A new heart I will give you, and a new spirit I will put within you; and I will take out of your flesh the heart of stone and give you a heart of flesh.

Ezekiel 36:26

Lord, come to us and take root in our lives. Help us to grow in your likeness and to be worthy of the new spirit that wells up within us.

ON BEING DISCHARGED

It's hot today, one of the dog days of August.
But it's a glorious day for us, Lord,
   a day of deliverance, of fitting conclusions.
Today, after five months of acute care,
   she leaves the hospital; she's discharged.
They have done all they can do for her here;
   it's time to move on.

The children and I brought in her clothes
   and helped her dress—no more hospital gowns!
Then we took her around to say goodbye
   to everyone who had cared for her for so long—
   the nurses in ICU, the therapists,
   the various physicians, even the security guards.
She made a point to say goodbye and thank you
   to each and every one.

Then we wheeled her out to the car
   where our dog was waiting to greet her return
   to the real world.
He jumped on her lap and licked her face
   as if she had never left.
"It's so bright out here," she said. "I can't see,"
   as the sun shone in her eyes.
"It's noisy too; it hurts my ears," she added,
   as the sounds of the city echoed around her.

Lord, she's back after a long, long absence.
Some of what she's missed is good and some is bad.
But it's all part of my world, God.
And I'm so thankful that she is back
   and part of it once again.
Whatever she missed, good or bad,
   can never compare to how badly I've missed her.

For thou hast delivered my soul from death,
    yea, my feet from falling,
that I may walk before God
    in the light of life.

Psalm 56:13

*Lord, thank you for those decisive moments in life when
we know beyond question that your will has been done.*

GOING TO
THE REHABILITATION CENTER

Her freedom was shortlived, God;
   today she goes to the rehabilitation center.
I've packed her clothing and personal things
   and loaded them, and her, into the car.
It's as if I'm taking her off to camp,
   just as I did with the children every summer.

As we arrive the aides take her to her room
   while I fill out forms and answer questions
   and meet the staff: new doctors and therapists.
I go through the process, God, and suddenly realize
   that I am giving her up all over again,
   just like before, and I am terror stricken—
   if only for a moment.
I don't want to lose her again—ever.
But I do want her to get better,
   to regain the confidence and strength she once had
   to look the world squarely in the eye.
And I know she needs to spend some time
   in a place like this to do that.

Lord, calm my fears and let me trust in you.
Give me the assurance that even though
   this is not exactly what I want for myself,
   it is what I want for her,
   and what she needs for herself
   to continue to progress toward
   the healing and wholeness you promise us all.

Give thanks in all circumstances; for this is the will
of God in Christ Jesus for you.

              1 Thessalonians 5:18

Lord, make us ever mindful of your guiding power in our lives, and help us to follow your wisdom even if it differs from ours.

A WEEKEND PASS

She has her first weekend pass from the center, Lord,
  the first two consecutive days we've had together
  in six months.

I parked at the front entrance of the building
  and went up the stairs to get her—
  her clothes and her wheelchair and her walker.
I piled it all in the trunk and helped her
  into the front seat, and off we went together
  to search for new adventure.
She, however, decided to settle for pizza.

So presently we were sitting on a blanket
  in the park, on a warm October day,
  with the sun streaking through the autumn leaves,
  munching away on cheese and pepperoni.
"It's a great life," she said.
  "Can I stay with you tonight?"
"It is a great life," I said, "and, yes, you can."

Thank you, Lord, for weekend passes,
  for precious moments and lovely memories.
Thank you for time shared together
  that is sometimes precious in its brevity.
Thank you for the beauty of your world
  and the joy of savoring its experiences.
It's a great day, and a great life too.
Thank you.

Hear this, O Job;
  stop and consider the wondrous works of
    God. . . .

Out of the north comes golden splendor;
  God is clothed with terrible majesty.
                              Job 37:14, 22

*Thank you, God, for time well spent in considering the
wonders of your creation and sharing it with those whom
we love.*

THE LONG WAY HOME

We are on the road to recovery, Lord, I know that.
But it's strewn with so many obstacles
    I've never had to face before.
He still can't walk without my help.
His speech is still slurred,
    and sometimes he mixes his words up.
I don't hear well anyway, and I don't always
    understand what he's trying to say.
And then he gets so frustrated and angry,
    more at himself than at me.
It hurts me to be a part of this, God.
It wears me out, too; I wish I had half the energy
    these young therapists do.
But they're not with him all day like I am.

O Lord, let me stop my complaining and take time
    to rejoice in what we have in one another.
We are together again, he's back home,
    and he is getting better, however slowly.
Let me take solace and find strength in those
    precious moments when our eyes meet
    across the table
    and we exchange a silent word of love.
Let me give thanks for the reassuring touch
    of his hand once again on my cheek.
Let me know all is well with us,
    and we will overcome this and find our way home
    to you.

"Behold, God is my salvation;
    I will trust, and will not be afraid;

for the LORD GOD is my strength and my song,
    and he has become my salvation."

Isaiah 12:2

*God, in times of frustration and doubt, inspire us with
your vision and refresh us with heaven-sent energy to
endure and overcome our burdens, one day at a time.*

LOSING FRIENDS

God, it's hard to face this;
    I've noticed it over the past few months.
Some of our longtime friends make fewer visits
    and they last for shorter lengths of time.
And I've noticed, too, Lord, that
    our times together aren't good times anymore.
They seem to feel uncomfortable around us both.
They sit awkwardly on their chairs
    with forced smiles on their faces.
Their carefully chosen words
    make for polite conversation.
But I can see they are hiding their true feelings.

One man my husband used to work with
    called to say he couldn't come over again.
He couldn't, he said, because seeing my husband
    upset him too much.
At least he was honest, Lord,
    but it didn't lessen my resentment,
    and I really didn't hide my feelings too well.
I told him that something like this
    should be a test of friendship, not a threat to it,
    and that being a friend is not to be taken lightly
    and then discarded in time of trouble.

I suppose, Lord, that illnesses are not the kind
    of things that some of us can share.
It does upset us—those who are healthy and well—
    to see those of us who are not.
And more than that I know it makes us face up
    to the fact that pain and suffering
    lie ahead in each of our lives.

God, help us to face up to ourselves,
    our strengths and weaknesses,
    our doubts and fears.
Help us to live with ourselves and one another
    and trust in your providence
    to make and keep us well.

This is my commandment, that you love one another as
I have loved you. Greater love has no man than this,
that a man lay down his life for his friends.

John 15:12–13

*Lord, help us to accept the frailties of our own nature,
so we can learn to love each other's weaknesses with all
of your strength that lies within us.*

THE SUPPORT GROUP

God, for a couple of weeks now
   I've been attending the support group meetings
   for stroke survivors and their families.
We all meet together for the first hour
   and then we split into separate groups—
   families in one room and survivors in another.

The first hour is cordial enough; we all talk
   about the progress our loved ones are making.
It's the second hour that things come unraveled
   when our "loved ones" leave the room.
That's when the complaints start, and the anger
   and the frustration come out.
I sit and listen, God, to the other wives talk,
   along with the husbands, parents, and children,
   and I feel angry at them for what they say
   and ashamed at myself for feeling the same way.
I want to blurt out, "What about them?
   How can you feel as you do?
   Look at yourselves—you're all healthy.
   You're not victims like they are."
And then I realize that we are—
   we are victims too.
Not in the same way, perhaps,
   but we have been stricken as well.
We have the right to feel as we do
   and the need to share that with one another.

The leader, a psychologist at the hospital,
   says this is right and the way it should be—
   to confront and deal with our feelings—
   or they may never go away
   and they will certainly get worse.

I think he's right, Lord—
   it feels good to me even when it hurts.
I am learning to live with my anger and resentment
   and not to feel guilty about it.
It's the only way to live, God.
Thanks for the support group.
Thanks for the support.

And let us consider how to stir up one another to love
and good works, not neglecting to meet together, as is
the habit of some, but encouraging one another, and all
the more as you see the Day drawing near.

Hebrews 10:24–25

*Thank you for the love and acceptance of others, Lord,
which allows us to be honest with ourselves.*

SEXUAL FRUSTRATION

When we were younger, we hardly had time for sex.
And when we took the time it was a hurried thing;
    we just went through the act
    and neither of us really enjoyed it.
Now the children are gone and the house is empty.
We have lots of time and lots of freedom
    but since he's had the stroke
    there isn't any interest.
It's so painful, Lord, not being wanted by him,
    not being desired or feeling desirable.
I miss what intimacy we did share,
    holding him close to me, being one with him
    and knowing that we are one together.
God, I want to literally feel that again
    as well as to know it.
I want to feel it in my body and in my soul.
I miss him, God; I love him and want him
    and I want him to want me.
You made us, Lord, male and female;
    you created us together.
You made us to love—to touch and join together.
Please, Lord, help us to do again
    what we were made for;
    help us to love each other.

But from the beginning of creation, "God made them male and female. For this reason a man shall leave his father and mother and be joined to his wife, and the two shall become one flesh. So they are no longer two but one flesh. What therefore God has joined together, let no man put asunder."

Mark 10:6–9

Lord, keep us from being rejected and alone and help us to face our feelings and share our intimate moments with those we love and believe we can trust.

GETTING IN THE DAY PROGRAM

I had our first interview with the people
   who run the day program, Lord.
This will be her third rehabilitation experience
   and the third time I've had to tell the story
   and convince the powers that be that my wife
   is a suitable candidate for their efforts.

The scenario is always the same—
   we make the cordial hellos;
   I explain our situation;
   they read her medical history
   and express their doubts about
   whether they can help her.
And then I have to recount all that she's done
   in previous therapy programs—
   how she's surprised everyone
   and exceeded all their expectations;
   how quickly she learned to walk again
   and how her memory has improved.

Lord, it all becomes so tedious,
   this negotiating and posturing back and forth.
What I'd really like to tell them
   is how she can help them if they would let her.
She could help to inspire them, God,
   give them new hope and vision in their work.
She could show them that even here,
   where suffering and pain go with the job,
   where progress is measured in inches,
   beautiful and miraculous things can happen.
She could do that for them, Lord;
   all they have to do is meet her.
And to do that,
   all they have to do is ask.

What shall I render to the LORD
   for all his bounty to me?
                              Psalm 116:12

*Lord, help us to recognize the true and lasting gifts of life
as they come from your bounty and grace.*

GOING TO THE DAY PROGRAM

The people in the day program met her, God.
They saw for themselves what I had told them,
    and then they accepted her
    just like I knew they would.

We bought new clothes, notebook, pen and paper,
    and packed a lunch for her first day.
It is as if I am taking my daughter off
    to her first day of school all over again.
I take her in at nine o'clock
    and pick her up at three.
She has classes in the morning
    to improve her memory and living skills
    and then physical therapy in the afternoon.
That's how I remember it myself—
    reading, writing, and arithmetic in the morning
    and gym class after lunch.

Life does run in cycles, God;
    what goes around comes around again.
Help us to remember that,
    so we don't keep making the same mistakes.
Help us to learn from our experiences
    and know you are always there to guide us—
    in the beginning, the middle, and the end.
Help us to trust in your judgment, God,
    even when we doubt our own.

By faith Abraham obeyed when he was called to go out
to a place which he was to receive as an inheritance; and
he went out, not knowing where he was to go.

Hebrews 11:8

God, keep us forever safe in your everlasting power and love and guide us in the decisions we make for ourselves and those whom we love.

THE WALKING WOUNDED

Our support group met last evening, Lord.
Our leader began by reading an article
   about stroke survivors and their difficulties.
He went on reading until he got to a part where
   stroke victims were called "the walking wounded"—
   and then he stopped and asked what we thought.

Some people felt the title was appalling,
   and we should never think that way about
   anyone trying to become healthy and whole again.
Someone else said it sounded all right;
   that it was an apt way to describe stroke victims
   and we shouldn't be so sensitive and indignant.
Finally, after some hesitation, a newer member
   of the group, who never spoke before, responded:
   "I think I'm part of the walking wounded too—
   my husband had a stroke, and he's recovered,
   eighty percent, but what about the other twenty?
   That's what I have to live with."

I can imagine how she does, Lord.
I have to live without my twenty percent too—
   the memory lapses, the upsets, the fall-downs.
I know the long hours of care and attention
   that we have to give.
I've walked in her shoes.
Her wounds are right where mine are.

You know too, Lord,
   and you know we're all in this together.
So come again, Lord;
   come and heal our wounds
   and help us walk with pride.

Count it all joy, my brethren, when you meet various trials, for you know that the testing of your faith produces steadfastness. And let steadfastness have its full effect, that you may be perfect and complete, lacking in nothing.

James 1:2–4

Lord, may the wounds we suffer and the trials we endure work to make us strong and fit to meet the challenges of life. May we stand steadfast and be triumphant over suffering.

RESPITE CARE

We went to the doctor for his checkup, God.
He's doing very well—
    his blood pressure and pulse are fine,
    his gait and speech are improving,
    and the doctor is very pleased.

After the exam the doctor asked my husband
    to see his nurse a moment
    and asked me to stay behind.
We sat across the desk; I sensed his apprehension
    and asked him what was wrong.
Fearing something about my husband,
    I was ready to hear the worst
    until I heard him talking about me instead.
He said I looked worn and tired and needed a rest,
    a respite from my duties.
He prescribed one day a week away—
    from my troubles, my responsibilities,
    and my husband.
He gave me the name of a respite care program
    at the local senior center.

God, I guess I can't hide the fact
    that I often look like I feel,
    and that's not so good at times.
In the midst of taking care of him
    I forget that I need care too.
So now, one day a week,
    a gentleman comes calling at my door,
    but not to call on me.
He's there to see my husband, to pass the day
    while I'm out and about taking care of myself.

"Run at once to meet her, and say to her, Is it well with you? Is it well with your husband? Is it well with the child?" And she answered, "It is well."

2 Kings 4:26

Thank you, Lord, for the time-outs of life—for holidays, vacations, and time away. Refresh us with your spirit and keep us well so that we may return to the duties that are ours and to those for whom we may be responsible.

"I DON'T REMEMBER"

Lord, I can recall the neurologist telling me,
   "This kind of stroke plays hell with the memory."
I didn't think about it at the time,
   but sometimes his words come back to haunt me.

I asked her if she turned off the stove
   and locked the kitchen door
   when we left the house last night.
She said she didn't remember.
I asked her today if she knew what happened
   to the checks I left on the desk.
She thought a moment and said,
   "I don't know; I don't remember."

Her memory is playing hell with my patience, God.
   I have enough to contend with
   without having to think for her all the time.
I remember that old phrase,
   "I'd like to give her a piece of my mind."
I think I would actually try it at the moment;
   maybe it would help.
I can back away from her and see real improvement,
   but it can be such a struggle for me sometimes.
I know she tries to do her best,
   but, Lord . . . so do I.
Please give me strength along the way,
   and accept the best from both of us.
And please, God, along the way,
   do your best for each of us.

But the fruit of the Spirit is love, joy, peace, patience, kindness, goodness, faithfulness, gentleness, self-control; against such there is no law.

Galatians 5:22–23

Lord of life, open our hearts to you, and may our faith be known in words of hope and acts of love: first to you and then to those around us.

DOWN TIME

Everyone has their down time, God, even her,
  and she's such a positive person.
Sometimes, though, it's impossible for me
  to keep her spirits up.

I read about a woman whose son suffered a stroke.
At one point in his recovery he was so depressed
  she had to hide his car keys and razor blades.
She and her husband couldn't let him
  out of their sight for weeks at a time;
  they were on watch day and night.
God, I am thankful we have never had to do that,
  but we do have our bleak moments.
Sometimes I see her sitting motionless in a chair,
  staring at the floor with this blank look on her face.
She seems vacant, as if she weren't there,
  so far removed from the world she once knew.
It hurts me, Lord, to see her this way,
  because I know she mourns her loss
  and there's nothing I can do to make it right.

Lord, only you can reach the depths of despair
  that a human heart can feel.
Only you can lift us up when we are down
  and draw us out of our time of gloom.
So come to us, God, with your good cheer
  and your assurance that life
  will be bright and beautiful again.

In that day you will ask nothing of me. Truly, truly, I
say to you, if you ask anything of the Father, he will
give it to you in my name.

John 16:23

God, we know there are no quick and easy answers to the problems we encounter, and we can be so easily overwhelmed. Keep us always in your care and lift us up above our tribulations when we have truly had enough.

GETTING LOST

She wanted to take another walk today.
  "Just around the block," she said.
  "I promise I won't get lost."
Sometimes it's up the street to the corner store,
  or one block beyond that to the church,
where she can go in and sit down for a while.
Sometimes she does get lost along the way.

I was so afraid last week, Lord,
  when she went out for a walk.
She was gone for thirty minutes
  and it was getting dark.
Our neighborhood isn't safe at night,
  and she was by herself for over an hour—
  alone and lost.
I called some friends and then the police
  to help find her.
The search went on for a long time.
Finally, a car drove up in front of our house.
My wife stepped out of the car and waved hello.
A friend of hers who doesn't even live nearby
  recognized her walking along a thoroughfare
  two miles from here and brought her home.

God, I just can't control everything.
I can't be with her all the time,
  and I can't lock her up like a house pet.
She had a stroke, but she's still a person
  and has the right to live her own life
  and go out when she feels like it.
God, keep her safe and out of harm's way.
Watch over her when I can't or she won't let me,
  and watch over me.

Sometimes I need all the help that you
   and everyone else can give
   to keep me from getting lost, too.

The LORD will keep you from all evil;
   he will keep your life.
The LORD will keep
   your going out and your coming in
   from this time forth and for evermore.
                    Psalm 121:7–8

Eternal God, thank you for your providential care in each of our lives; help us to know that you are always with us, even when we feel most alone.

GETTING HIS LICENSE BACK

I can't say I've been looking forward to this,
  certainly not as much as he has.
He goes for his driving test today, Lord.
He took some lessons from an instructor
  who works with older people
  recovering from illnesses such as stroke.

He passed his written test already;
  he only missed three questions out of thirty.
He got confused over who has the right-of-way
  at an intersection with four stop signs.
I had to admit I was confused myself.
He passed his vision and reflex tests, too.
He sat in front of lots of machines
  and pressed buttons and stepped on pedals.
It reminded me of video games our grandson plays
  when he goes to the mall.

So here we are, Lord, the big test
  behind the wheel.
I really don't know who's more anxious.
And I really don't know what we'll do
  if he doesn't do well here.
Lord, be with my husband whenever he drives,
  but be with him especially in this moment.
The examiner is coming now;
  he looks calm enough—even bored,
  but then he does this every day.
My husband doesn't,
  and while he's always been an excellent driver,
  he hasn't had to prove it in forty years.

Help him drive safely, God, and convince us all
  that he deserves to get his license back.

"Therefore I tell you, do not be anxious about your life, what you shall eat or what you shall drink, nor about your body, what you shall put on. Is not life more than food, and the body more than clothing?"

Matthew 6:25

God, calm our anxieties and fears when we have to assert ourselves for what we know is right.

GOING OUT ON A DATE

"I want to go out on a date," she said.
"I'll wear my new dress;
   we'll have dinner and go dancing,
   just like we did before the stroke."
I planned the evening carefully—
   a little champagne before we left,
   a small gift for her on the coffee table,
   reservations at our favorite restaurant.

It's nice, Lord, to be able to rekindle some
   romantic notions of the past.
We had a wonderful time.
Dinner was superb, just like always,
   with candlelight and wine.
Dancing was a bit more subdued.
Before her stroke she'd clear the floor
   and everyone would watch.
This time, though, I held her close
   just in case she lost her balance.
She enjoyed it even more, she said,
   because now she only wanted to dance with me.

I had a marvelous time, God—
   the best date I can remember.
Thank you both for a lovely evening;
   I hope we can do it again soon.

Truly, truly, I say to you, you will weep and lament, but
the world will rejoice; you will be sorrowful, but your
sorrow will turn into joy.

                             John 16:20

We praise you, God, for those splendid moments when everything goes right for us. Thank you for bringing joy out of our sorrow and making our lives complete.

A MEDLEY OF FEELINGS

Sometimes, Lord, I wish I didn't think
  and feel the way I do.
I'm not made of stone; I'm human like the rest
  and I have some very human feelings.

I lie next to her in bed at night, awake,
  and start to think and begin to feel as I do.
I think about her coma and miraculous awakening,
  and I feel the sense of awe all over again.
I think about her deficits,
  and I feel guilty because I am whole
  and she is not—at least not yet.
I sometimes think about our life now
and am angry at you because I'm still alone,
and at her because she left me—
even though it's not her fault.
God, I am so confused in these dark hours
  I don't know what to do, or what I feel,
  or how to settle or reconcile myself.
I think, Lord, you are the only one
  who can do that for me.

Come to me, God, in the still of the night.
Calm my soul and reconcile my humanity,
  with its conflicts and confusion,
  with your gracious holy spirit.

But when you pray, go into your room and shut the
door and pray to your Father who is in secret; and your
Father who sees in secret will reward you.

                               Matthew 6:6

God, as we do battle with the perplexities and gray areas of our daily lives, come to us in those private moments, hear our pleas for enlightenment, and grant us clarity and wisdom.

FUTURE WISHES AND EXPECTATIONS

What do I wish for the future? What do I expect?
I wish he would return to normal, God,
    except for a few annoying habits
    I never really liked.
I wish our lives could be the same—
    except that we could afford a few more things.
I wish we could learn more from this experience
    and never count the cost.
I wish I had more strength and patience
    from living through his stroke,
    and could forget all the pain it took
    to gain what I have so far.

I expect though, Lord, that not all of this will happen.
For as much as I would like to believe it,
    the future never comes if you deny the past.
You don't know what the future holds
    if you don't know you have one.
I expect, after all we have been through,
    that we will not forget.

I hope, Lord, you will guide us into the future
    confident and unafraid,
    and we will both remember
    what it took to get us there.

For there is nothing hid, except to be made manifest;
nor is anything secret, except to come to light.

Mark 4:22

We thank you, Lord, for the past even as we face the future. We thank you that it is your will that all things should be made known to us so we may live a life of faithfulness.

FIVE

AFFIRMATION
OF LIFE

WHAT HAVE I LEARNED FROM THIS?

Ever since I was a child I have been taught
 that every experience is an opportunity to learn.
We profit through well-deserved triumph;
 virtue is its own reward.
We benefit from every adversity;
 suffering is redemptive.
What have I learned from this experience, God?
What have I gained from suffering
 through this stroke?

I have learned patience, learned how to wait.
I have learned humility
 and learned how not to be so self-assured.
I have come to realize the limitations
 of my physical prowess and emotional strength
 to endure undue hardship, Lord.
And I have gained a greater dependence on you,
 an awareness that it is OK to ask for help,
 along with the knowledge that you really don't
 burden us with more than we can handle.

It may sound trite when I say this, God,
 but it is also just as true.
I've grown older through this experience,
 and as I have grown older
 I have grown wiser and more content.
Wise enough to know that there is
 much more for me to learn,
 and content enough to let you teach me
 in your own good time.

For I am sure that neither death, nor life, nor angels,
nor principalities, nor things present, nor things to

come, nor powers, nor height, nor depth, nor anything else in all creation, will be able to separate us from the love of God in Christ Jesus our Lord.

Romans 8:38–39

Lord, teach us to always trust in your wisdom and keep faith with your promise to always be with us.

A CHAT WITH SALLIE

Sallie is my wife's respiratory therapist.
I met her, like everyone else at the hospital,
   in the midst of an emergency
   when we all believed my wife was going to die.
From the very outset
   I was struck with her kindness and compassion.
She was the only one I saw outside the hospital.
In fact, we met one day at another one across town.
I was visiting a friend.
She was visiting her husband.
My friend, like my wife, recovered, Lord.
Sallie's husband came home from the hospital,
   and then he went back in and died.
All the time that Sallie was trying to save
   my wife's life, her husband was losing his.
There was nothing she could do for him,
   but it went on all that time and I never knew.

I spoke with Sallie today;
   she wanted to know how we were.
I was so touched by her call I wanted to reach out
   and hug her through the phone.
We had a special bond, Sallie and I.
Some would say I suffered and won, God,
   and she suffered and lost.
But I say she's a winner if you ever made one.

Thank you, God, for Sallie.
Thank you for putting people like her
   in places where they can help people like us.

And the King will answer them, "Truly, I say to you, as you did it to one of the least of these my brethren, you did it to me."

Matthew 25:40

Thank you, God, for compassionate people who follow your call in putting other people's needs ahead of their own. May we learn to become more like them.

DINNER WITH THE CHILDREN

It was quite a celebration,
   her first birthday at home after her stroke.
We had a big dinner with all the children.
She asked for lobster; I could only afford it
   for her; the children looked on in envy.

As we sat around the table, Lord,
   laughing and talking all at the same time,
   I noticed we have all gotten older this year.
I look at the children and see they have grown.
Each one is different,
   pursuing their own aspirations in their lives.
They are more their own persons now,
   surer of themselves and less dependent on us.
They are also more separate from us, more alone.
Sometimes I feel a great distance between us,
   tempered by tragic loss and sudden change.

For all the promise of new life, Lord,
   I can't quite overlook the past.
I wasn't ready for the children
   to grow up as quickly as they did.
But I realize they weren't ready either
   and did it only because they had to.
Still I miss them, God.
I miss them as children
   sitting around the table
   laughing and talking all at the same time
   over dinner with their mother.

For everything there is a season, and a time for every matter under heaven . . . a time to weep, and a time to laugh; a time to mourn, and a time to dance.

Ecclesiastes 3:1, 4

O God, help me to accept the changes in my life: to let go of times past, and look toward times to come, and to realize that our times are in your hands.

VOLUNTEER WORK

Each day brings something new for him, God—
   a new opportunity, a new acquaintance.
For so many years he was dedicated to his work
   and frustrated by the idea
   that he never provided for us as he wanted to.

Now it's all changed;
   he volunteers his time and energy
   and I've never seen him so happy.
One day he delivers meals to the elderly,
   the next he works at a senior center,
   and on another day he works at church
   helping our pastor.
Each day he tells me what he's learned,
   and each day is a learning experience for me too.
I watch him improve and share in his enthusiasm,
   and I realize that giving to others
   is the best way to make yourself whole.

Thank you, God, that he can give of himself to others.
Thank you, God, for what he gives to me.

Heal the sick, raise the dead, cleanse lepers, cast out demons. You received without paying, give without pay.

Matthew 10:8

Help us to learn, Lord, that it is in giving to others as you give to us that we receive more than we give.

LOOKING BACK AND LOOKING FORWARD

Lord, it is getting better all the time.
He's made real progress
    in regaining his strength and abilities.
I am learning to accept his weaknesses.
I would never have believed it,
    but I actually see good coming out of this.
We were always so busy before, so consumed
    by our own wants and needs.
And it's no secret to either of us that sometimes
    we pursued them at each other's expense.
And then each of us would make the other
    feel guilty for resenting our actions.

But now, God, we see how good life can be for us
    and how much we mean to one another.
Now, after all these years, we know what it is
    to give freely, receive happily,
    and truly love someone.
I've often heard our pastor say,
    "Suffering is redemptive."
But I never realized what that meant. How could I?
I never knew what suffering really was
    until these past few months.
There was so much pain and darkness;
    I don't know how I stood it.

But now I know what it means to "redeem the time."
It means you came to make all things
    bright and new for us, Lord,
    and for everyone who needs your healing power.
Thank you, Lord. Thank you, forever.

Every good endowment and every perfect gift is from above, coming down from the Father of lights with whom there is no variation or shadow due to change.
James 1:17

Eternal God, make us ever mindful of your gracious love for us. Let us praise your name now and forever.

A TOAST TO A NEW LIFE TOGETHER

"I'd like to propose a toast," she said,
    "to you, to me, and to God."
I listened and nodded my assent, Lord.
But I also wondered to myself:
    Have you been toasted lately?
I raised my fist and cursed you in the darkness.
Now she comes to make it up to you and
    make all things new.

How do you feel, God, about our raising glasses
    to you by candlelight as we celebrate the victory
    and rejoice in the promise of a new life together?
I don't think you need to
be appeased, God.
I think you'd rather celebrate with us
    and join in the toast.
Your toast is your testament to us, God,
    that we have been redeemed
    and called by name into a new life together.
Thanks be to you, O Lord, for giving us the victory.

And I heard a loud voice from the throne saying, "Behold, the dwelling of God is with men. He will dwell with them, and they shall be his people, and God himself will be with them; he will wipe away every tear from their eyes, and death shall be no more, neither shall there be mourning nor crying nor pain any more, for the former things have passed away."

And he who sat upon the throne said, "Behold, I make all things new." Also he said, "Write this, for these words are trustworthy and true."

Revelation 21:3–5

Lord, we know your words are true. Thank you that the mourning has passed away, just as you said it would, and thank you now for all things new.

FAITH

Faith is fidelity to a cause,
   a confidence in something beyond ourselves.
Having faith is believing in what we cannot see,
   holding on to what we cannot feel,
   affirming what we cannot prove.
Keeping faith is our calling,
   which comes from you, God;
   it's believing in what you show us to be real,
   holding on to what you give us for safekeeping,
   and relying on what you tell us as the truth.
We respond to our calling by placing our trust
   in you, the author of our faith.
But what happens when faith fails us?
What becomes of our trust when it is broken?

You give us faith and we keep it with you—
   faith is a two-way street.
But who keeps the faith in times of doubt and crisis,
   is it us or is it you?
Our faith without a doubt is often untried.
Our faith with serious doubt is sometimes untrue.
Your faith, God, is the faith that moves mountains.
Your faith sustains us in all times and places;
   even in the darkest nights of our souls
   we see that you were there with us all along.

Join us, God.
Join us in faith.
Join us in faith and life together.

Now faith is the assurance of things hoped for, the conviction of things not seen.

Hebrews 11:1

Create a longing within us, O Lord, that we may be more able to live a life of faithfulness, not counting the cost.

HOPE

Hope is a promise that has yet to be fulfilled,
    and the expectation that it soon will be.
Hope evolves from a fleeting feeling
    to sureness that events will turn out for the best,
    that what is desired is also possible.
Hope springs eternal for it comes from you, God.
With you there is no fading, no ending of hope.

In times of trouble, Lord, we look to you for hope;
    we seek your way and hope it's the way to peace.
Yet our hope is such a fragile thing;
    it depends so much on faith
    which is so fragile in itself.
Our hope is elusive:
    we want to hope but aren't sure how;
    we hope for the best in the worst of times
    and then wonder what is best.

Show us your way, Lord, and do for us
    what you know is best.
Reveal yourself to us.
Make your face to shine upon us
    and increase our hope.

For in this hope we were saved. Now hope that is seen
is not hope. For who hopes for what he sees? But if we
hope for what we do not see, we wait for it with patience.

                                                Romans 8:24–25

*God, make us to know that hope is more than a pleasing
impulse; let us see it as a harbinger of your redemptive
love.*

LOVE

The essence of love is a simple truth
  I learned in childhood, God:
You are love.
And we love you,
  but only because you loved us first.

Your love is kind and tenderhearted, Lord;
  it is slow to lose patience;
  its hope never falters; it never lets us go.
Your love is awesome and powerful;
  it is a force to be reckoned with, never static;
  it never lets us get away.
Your love is gracious:
  we haven't earned it, we don't deserve it,
  and we can never turn it down.
You choose to love us;
You follow hard after us to give us the good news
  that we are acceptable to you,
  that we are quintessentially good, and
  that you desire us with a passionate aspiration.

We see you standing at the crossroads and crises
  of our lives, God.
Your arms are outstretched and waiting
  to welcome us into your household
  and offer us a haven of safety and rest.
You have set the example for us, God.
You have shown us the way.
Let us follow then in the way of love.

Beloved, if God so loved us, we also ought to love one
another. No man has ever seen God; if we love one
another, God abides in us and his love is perfected in

us. . . . There is no fear in love, but perfect love casts out fear. . . . So we know and believe the love God has for us. God is love, and he who abides in love abides in God, and God abides in him.

1 John 4:11–12, 18a, 16

God, we praise your name and thank you for your love. It knows no limit to its endurance, no end to its trust, no fading of its hope. It is the one thing that still stands when all else has fallen. Show us this love, God, that we may show it to others, and may your grace be with us all.

ADDITIONAL RESOURCES

The following books provide excellent help in understanding the causes and effects of stroke from the lay point of view.

Hess, Lucille J., and Robert E. Bahr. *What Every Family Should Know About Strokes.* New York: Appleton-Century-Crofts, 1981.
   Contains its own bibliography, along with references to companies and agencies providing stroke services through the courts.

Lavin, John H. *Stroke: From Crisis to Victory—A Family Guide.* New York: Franklin Watts, 1985.
   Traces the history of stroke in a particular family from its onset through recovery and also contains a glossary of terms pertaining to stroke.

Sarno, John E., and Martha Taylor Sarno. *Stroke: A Guide for Patients and Their Families.* Rev. ed. New York: McGraw-Hill Book Co., 1979.
   Provides vital information on strokes, arranged in a readable question-and-answer format.